The Elements of
Self-Improvement

The Elements of Self-Improvement

Adrian Phillips

Black Point Publishing
Vancouver, B.C., Canada

Published in 2012 by
Black Point Publishing
Vancouver, B.C., Canada
www.Elements-of-Self-Improvement.com

ISBN 978-0-9880352-0-1 paperback
ISBN 978-0-9880352-0-8 hardcover
ISBN 978-0-9880352-2-5 eBook

Contents

GETTING STARTED

Self-improvement. We all strive for it. Most of us use the same approach: We learn from experience and by observing others – mimicking their successes and learning from their trials and errors. Imitation may be the sincerest form of flattery, but its better use is to help us get ahead.

What impedes self-improvement? Four factors stand out: a lack of time for enough trials, errors, and wins; a lack of personal experience; a shortage of exposure to the success of others; and forgetting to use what we have learned from valuable lessons.

This book is a collection of distilled "goods" gained from the experiences of many successful people in many different situations. The content of this book is broad. It lists many behaviors to emulate, many rules to follow, and several things to avoid. The collection period (my collection period) spans more than 30 years. You may find that it takes you 30 years to put all or even some of these recommendations to use.

Use this book as a box of tools for achieving success. You may employ a number of the tools immediately; some not for several years, and then maybe only once; and some, never. Use each of the tools as a situation may require – you may end up using certain ones over and over again. You will likely get the most from this book by reading all of it now, and then setting it aside for future reference.

I

The Basics

7 building blocks

1. **Do a few things and do them well** – You have a limited amount of time, energy, wealth, and intellect. Use these resources wisely by dedicating them to a small number of pursuits. Keep your standards very high. Remember that a jack-of-all-trades is a master of none.

2. **Craft and guard your reputation** – A good reputation comes with time and a lot of hard work. It is one of your top assets. However, it can be easy to lose – sometimes from one foolish or thoughtless act or misjudgment. Once it's gone, you cannot buy it back and you may never earn it back. Life is simpler and more prosperous when you have a good reputation. Build one and protect it.

3. **Stick to principles for the long term** – Always conduct your personal and professional affairs in the highest moral, ethical, and rigorous fashion. You will do so many things in life that you will forget the details of many of them. However, when you are held accountable for an action that you may not even recall, you will not want to waste energy retracing or recreating or glossing over what has been brought to light. You can withstand any challenge if you are able to state, with certainty, that you never knowingly broke the rules, did an incomplete job, or skirted an issue.

4. Develop breadth by joining at least one social organization – Regular involvement with a group of people outside family and work is important. This may be a religious organization, sports team, activity club, or any similar group. These outings will give you a broader sense of humanity and a deeper sense of humility.

5. Donate to the "cosmic charity" – Helping others often results in a benefit to you at some point in the future. This simply means helping someone who is in need when there is nothing in it for you.

A senior executive (also a good friend) once helped a fellow employee who needed personal assistance. Many years later the employee remembered this kindness and recommended my friend to her husband, who was recruiting for an executive placement. He tracked my friend down and invited him to take part in the interviewing process. Within weeks he became the Chief Executive Officer of a $400-million corporation.

While this appears highly coincidental, countless stories like this link one good turn to another. Live by the practice of committing random acts of kindness.

6. Follow an active reading program – This is one of the simplest and most effective ways to improve yourself, yet it is highly convenient, enjoyable, and relaxing, and it requires no special equipment or effort by others. Ever heard the expression "you are what you eat"? You are also what you read. Read as much as you can.

Reading provides three major benefits:

(i) It hones your ability to communicate in all forms (including speaking and writing)

(ii) It increases the depth and breadth of your knowledge

(iii) It enhances your ability to absorb information

Dedicate your reading to materials that provide these benefits. Place more emphasis on history, science, arts, religion, commerce, biography, and related topics. Read fewer fictional and entertainment works. This is not a recommendation to read textbooks only but to seek learning experiences through an enjoyable pastime.

You might focus on reading about people who started with nothing and built something substantial. Include those who battled adversity, such as military figures or those with handicaps or deprived upbringings. Spend less time reading the biographies of lucky people who became famous or had a substantial head start via inheritances and the like. You may also find some great reading in novels grounded in important historical, scientific, or religious events.

Reading differs from almost all other forms of learning because you control the rate of intake. Radio, television, films, lectures, and even simple conversation deliver information at slower rates. Also, reading does not require specific equipment, preset viewing times, or special locations. The amount of topical material is hundreds, if not thousands, times larger than what is available from all other media.

Carry good reading materials with you at all times. Great reading opportunities often arise by surprise (such as when you are waiting for a delayed flight). You can make good use of what otherwise would be wasted time. Always, always, always carry reading material with you.

7. Evolve in five areas of focus – The five main areas of focus that contribute to the success of people through their school years and into their early adult years are sports, arts, academics, part-time or summer jobs, and volunteering.

While these are broad categories, the point is to become very good at one or two of these activities while participating in the other areas for balance. Work hard on getting high grades in your studies. Tackle some jobs as a laborer or in retail sales or food service. Contribute to the greater community by being part of student government and by helping the infirm or the less privileged. Why? Because these activities and experiences will make you a better person.

What you learn during your earlier years will benefit you throughout your life.

Consider, for example, those seeking career opportunities after completing their formal education. Prospective employers will not be interested in just their experience or expertise. Rather, they will assess their ability to deliver to a high standard, perform under adversity, tackle complex tasks, contribute to team efforts, exhibit a broad level of appreciation, and compete and win. How do employers make this assessment? By reviewing how well the candidates have performed in non-work but real-life situations, such as on the court, in performances, in the classroom, or in the community.

This is not about building a strong résumé; it is about building a strong character. These qualities will shine through in interviews.

This approach does not have to stop at the end of your formal education. Focusing on these areas into your midlife years and later will provide ongoing benefits.

7 key warnings

8. Never say never – Avoid saying, or doing, things that may limit your future ability to maneuver. Do not box yourself in with an irreversible statement. Saying "I will never …" may limit your ability to make an important course correction because you fear being embarrassed if you don't live up to your grand statement.

Similarly, predictions that someone will never do something or that something will never happen are typically proved wrong. How many politicians have firmly stated "no new taxes" only to have to eat those words later at great cost to their reputations? Avoid limiting yourself, and always remain aware that people and situations, no matter how intractable they appear, will eventually change.

9. Assume that anything could end up as front-page news – Very few, if any, of your actions will remain a secret, no matter how hard you may try to keep them that way. People constantly pay witness to what you do. Then they talk about it.

The good news is that many will be aware of, and discuss, your good deeds. The bad news is that they will also be aware of, and discuss, your bad deeds.

Rather than waste energy by trying to cover up your weaker or dumber efforts, act such that anything you say or do could hit the front page of a newspaper (or be broadly circulated in a social network) and not limit your opportunities. Make this a daily practice; it will serve to protect one of your most valuable assets – your reputation.

10. **Do not be fooled by the low probability of danger** – You will sometimes be in situations where it is very unlikely that something bad will happen, but if it does, the repercussions could be serious.

Call this the "low probability of being shot in the heart." Drunk drivers who have killed others, daredevils who are now paraplegics, and petty thieves who have earned themselves a criminal record are all members of this club of unfortunates. Striving for a small benefit, such as avoiding the cost of a taxi by driving home after drinking because you believe you are unlikely to get caught (police nab only a fraction of drunk drivers) is simply not worth it. This is one club that you definitely do not want to join.

11. **Assume that criticism will not be kept secret** – People often make the mistake of thinking that their criticism of others will be kept secret or have little harm if it is not. Not true. Criticism typically makes its way to the "victim," with effects that are usually worse than the message you intended. Unfortunately, the transmission most certainly will have your name attached to it.

If you must criticize, do so face to face. Be gentle and fair and have a full discussion. Little is kept secret in social circles and the workplace. Being labeled a critic will be a drag on your advancement.

12. **Do not fight City Hall** – Put your efforts where there is at least some prospect of a reasonable return. Avoid bothering with situations over which you have little control or influence. It is worth adopting these words from the well-known prayer by Reinhold Niebuhr, which asks for the serenity to accept "the things that cannot be changed, courage to change the things which should be changed, and the wisdom to distinguish the one from the other."

13. **Do not be a living martyr** – Do not give too much of yourself for the benefit of others. If you perpetually help families, friends, and colleagues, you will be forced to ignore your own needs and will suffer as a result. Look after your own health, happiness, welfare, aspirations, and advancement. This foundation will actually strengthen your efforts to give to others.

14. **Place limits on alcohol; be very careful with recreational drugs** – Moderate use of alcohol and other recreational drugs can enhance the enjoyment of a social gathering. However, more is not better in this arena. Show too much personality during a party and you may be labeled a clown in the days that follow. Worse, displaying a chemically enhanced, larger-than-normal personality for no apparent reason will mark you as someone with a problem.

Some people place marijuana and other "soft" drugs in the same category as alcohol because the effects are similar. You may consider them interchangeable, but the law and the police see alcohol and drugs as distinctly different and will treat you accordingly. Many organizations have zero-tolerance policies toward drugs and conduct specific tests to make sure their people adhere to these policies.

Before using recreational drugs, consider the non-recreational effects of being caught. A minor drug possession conviction may be a badge of honor for a rap star, but it can be career-limiting to a church elder, attorney, and others.

II

Getting Better

1 rule for physical well-being

15. **Do what Mother Nature tells you** – How can you become healthy and physically fit? How can you avoid feeling tired, sick, and run down? The answer comes from a simple observation. Human beings have been on this planet in substantially the same form for the past 10,000 years. Although we are an evolving species that can adapt to new and different climates and food regimens, these changes take place over many generations and hundreds of years. The body is a complex biochemical system that has molded itself to fairly regular nutrition and activity patterns.

However, over the past century we have made substantial changes to the food we eat and the way we live. What are these changes? Eating processed foods, refined carbohydrates, and food chemicals not found in nature. Consuming caffeinated, carbonated, high-fat, or high-sugar beverages that are nothing like the liquids we drank during the previous 9,900 years. Going for days without lean proteins, grains, fruits, and vegetables when our digestive system is designed for daily doses of these food groups.

Consider as well that many of us get fewer vitamins and minerals than the amounts our ancestors derived from Mother Nature.

Do not forget other limiting factors, such as a reduced amount of sunlight and fresh air every day.

And how about a big reduction in physical activity? Not that long ago we were either hunters or farmers out in the sunshine and fresh air, burning off twice as many calories as we do today. If you are feeling down, it is probably because your body is being subjected to a regimen that is out of step with the best practices of our ancestors.

You can maximize your physical capabilities simply by mimicking the patterns of those ancestors. Eat unprocessed foods. Eat a balanced diet high in vegetables and grains, moderate in proteins, and low in fats, refined sugars, and processed foods. Drink lots of water. Get outdoors daily and adopt a vigorous exercise routine. Your body is not built for eating pizza at midnight, spending 24 hours a day in closed buildings, drinking booze by the bottle, living under artificial light, or going days without fresh vegetables.

Listen when your body sends you signals. Poor body function is a sign that some form of change is required. Ease back when vigorous activity or exercise produces acute pain. Do you have bad fingernails, terrible hair, gurgling guts, or sore gums? Do you have difficulty sleeping at night? Your body is sending you a clear signal that something is wrong and an adjustment is needed.

Get a good sleep every night. Our healthy ancestors did. You sleep for about one-third of your life. Make it count. Make sure your surroundings are comfortable. Buy a good mattress, not a cheap one. Sleeping is the act of recharging your mind and body for the next waking period. Do not shortchange yourself.

12 ways to look sharp

16. **Dress like your peers** – Wear conservative clothes if you live in a conservative world and flamboyant clothes if you live in a flamboyant one. Dress to blend in with your community.

17. **Dress one-half level better than your peers** – You will want to be noticed because you dress, groom, and handle yourself one-half level better than your peers. You do not want to be noticed because you are positioned at either extreme of the dress and grooming spectrum. Let us be clear: Many people judge a book by its cover. Dress, grooming, and hygiene are your cover. They are critical to the way you will be judged.

18. **Dress one-quarter level better than the occasion** – Your probability of regret is much higher if you under-dress than if you over-dress. This does not mean wearing a tux to a football game. It means wearing lace-up shoes when others are wearing loafers, wearing a skirt when others are wearing slacks, or wearing a collared shirt when others are in crew necks.

19. **Assemble a wardrobe that is essentially consistent** – Variety, yes; randomness, no. No matter how fashionable or high in quality it may be, a piece of clothing that stands out from what you typically wear will make people remember you as the person who wears that "unusual" outfit every second Tuesday.

20. Maintain your wardrobe – Attend to that loose thread, keep your shoes shiny, make sure your clothes are freshly ironed when they are supposed to look that way, and replace that lost button. If you look shabby, sloppy, worn down, disorganized, or disheveled, people may believe that *you* are shabby, sloppy, worn down, disorganized, or disheveled. These superficial assessments may well cost you future opportunities.

I once met a man who judged people's character partly on the state of their shoeshine. He was a senior executive and a decision maker who was capable of awarding several business contracts to our firm. The shininess of my shoes contributed a small but important part to our success in securing him as a very important and profitable client.

21. Avoid contradictory dressing – The sharp dresser will not be caught wearing long sleeve shirts with shorts, Oxford shoes with denim, two different plaids, or a brown belt with black shoes, not to mention textures that are mismatched to color and garment styles to fabric weight. If you do not understand how to coordinate clothing, get help.

22. Buy high-quality clothes – High-quality clothes look better and last longer. They are more comfortable and stay in style longer. You can spend the same money buying lots of cheap clothing or fewer items of high-quality clothing. This year's cheap clothes are next year's charity donations. This year's quality clothes are good for next year and possibly many to come. Over the long run, higher-quality clothes will cost you less.

23. **Stick to a color theme** – Having a wide variety of clothes means you have to match them. This can be expensive, both in time and money. If blue looks good on you, then build your wardrobe around blue. This does not mean that everything has to be blue or have blue in it; just make sure you buy clothes that are compatible with blue.

24. **Beware the deep discount sale** – Clothes that go on sale at very cheap prices are clothes that could not be sold to anyone at full price.

25. **Keep yourself neat** – Keep your nails clean and properly trimmed. Keep your hair trimmed and in style. Brush your teeth after every meal and avoid exposing people near you to specks of your lunch stuck in your teeth, or worse, bad breath. Apply creams to dry skin. Wash your hands often and get rid of any stains, paint, and grease from those messy projects.

26. **Groom yourself at home** – Nail clipping, hair plucking, skin defoliation, and blackhead squeezing should all be done in the privacy of your own quarters. People perform these functions in public or in a work area on the misguided assumption that nobody is looking. If you must attend to something for social acceptability, do not do so in a socially unacceptable way. Head for the washroom or some other 100% private setting.

27. **Avoid the Saturday special** – The quest for comfort can lead to lapses in responsible grooming. Avoid taking that Saturday outing with curlers in your hair. Do not show up without shaving. Do not board an airplane dressed for the privacy of your backyard. Every public outing warrants that you be reasonably groomed and attired. You may encounter a person or situation that will influence your future.

22 pointers on writing

One of the greatest skills is writing quickly and effectively.
The pen is mightier than the sword, and you will want to be
faster with the pen than with the sword. The physical writing
of a thought, recommendation, opinion, or even a simple
thank-you strengthens meaning and improves clarity. Written
words often deliver a stronger and longer-lasting impact than
spoken words.

Some ways to write quickly and easily:

28. **Do not force yourself to write things in order** – You
do not have to compose your work in the order that someone
will read it. Many writers get bogged down by trying to write
the introduction first, the body second, and the conclusion
last. You may wish to have a catchy opening line, but it is
not likely to pop into your head when you start a project.
Do not force yourself to write the key messages in the logical
order they will appear in the end. Generate all of the thoughts,
arguments, diagrams, etc., as they come to you, or as you wish
to tackle them, and *then* put them in logical order.
Many a great work is completed with the writing of
the introduction.

29. **Plan the takeaways** – People tend to distill what they read into a few very simple thoughts; you could call them takeaways. Decide the messages that you want to communicate and then design your writing around them. The need for key takeaway messages applies whether the piece is short or long.

30. **Remember that it is easier to edit than create** – Schools teach us that copying someone else's work is a bad thing. While this may be true for term papers, it is not true for everyday communications. Save, then re-use, examples of good writing. Do not hesitate to *imitate* someone else's style of wording, structural order, or imagery in your written pieces. Never *copy* somebody else's wording; that constitutes stealing their intellectual property. Using someone else's work as a first draft and then improving it (and changing the wording and even the message) can make writing wonderfully easy. Be careful, though. Some people end up plagiarizing because they forget to reword passages. Source material can range from a few of your own better-crafted pieces to magazine or journal articles to excerpts from the works of famous writers.

31. **Take the reader through a logical sequence** – Consider a written work to be like a lawyer's closing presentation to a judge or jury. Provide a brief introduction, the body of your message, and a brief conclusion. Place tables and graphs directly within your text to present a continuous flow of logic. Do not make the reader hopscotch through various sections of the document. Summarize information into a succinct list of points or use a graph or table. Then, but only if necessary, direct the more committed reader to a fuller treatment in a supplemental section such as an appendix.

32. **Arrange your work into three sections** – Writing is frequently used to persuade the reader of a certain point of view or to encourage a certain reaction. Most written works can be arranged into three sections. For a letter or memorandum, they are:

(i) A one- or two-sentence attention grabber that introduces the topic

(ii) The body, describing the facts, thesis, proposal, or main content

(iii) One or two sentences committing to an action or calling for a reaction

The three sections of a longer piece, such as an essay, research report, or flip-book presentation, are:

(i) A few sentences or a list describing the contents of the work

(ii) The body

(iii) A conclusion emphasizing what the reader should take away from the document

A common formula is "tell them what you are going to tell them, tell them, and then tell them what you have told them."

33. **Use snappy words** – Make your written works more memorable by using vibrant words and phrases. Saying someone is "riveted" to the television is more vivid than saying the person is "watching" the television. Similarly, if you can convey a meaning in a title, then do it. For example, "Eight Reasons Why You Should Donate to Our Charity" is a much more compelling heading for the last section of a brochure than "Summary and Conclusions."

34. **Employ facts and numbers** – Which of the following two cars would an informed buyer be more enticed to buy? A car that accelerates really fast, has a high top speed, corners well, and stops quickly, or one that goes from 0 to 60 mph in

5.5 seconds, can reach a speed of 165 mph, corners at 0.90 g, and stops from 60 mph to 0 mph in 105 feet? Facts and figures can make your presentation much more informative and convincing.

35. **Use short words and simple thoughts** – Do not think that you will impress a reader by using five-syllable words, 50-word sentences, and 50-sentence paragraphs. You will not. "The quick brown fox jumps over the lazy dog" says as much with fewer and simpler words as, "The expeditious brunette canid propels itself in an arc of elevated air travel above the canine that is not inclined to undertake ventures requiring substantial physical efforts."

36. **Place your message clearly at the beginning or the end of a paragraph** – A paragraph is a series of sentences that deliver a message. Do not make the reader hunt for the message. Put it in the first sentence of the paragraph and support it with the sentences that follow. Equally good is to build up your line of reasoning and then put your main point in the last sentence of the paragraph.

37. **Read it out loud** – Reading your own writing out loud is an excellent way to proofread it. This practice will help you thin out long sections, sort out confusing sentences, and correct your grammar.

Some things to avoid:

38. **Avoid writing to others when you are mad, sad, or stressed** – If you feel you have to react to a recent, negative event, prepare a draft and let it sit overnight. Rewrite it after you have had time for reflection and your emotions have softened. If you are forced to write something quickly to meet a deadline, ask a friend or colleague to proofread it. What you write when you are angry, frazzled, or excited will tend to over-emphasize emotion and under-emphasize important meaning. Those who fire off a written communication often end up regretting unintended responses and consequences.

39. Do not describe water to a drowning man – Written materials should provide the reader with a useable product. Other than when you are writing descriptive pieces for travel brochures or catalogues, your message should inform, explain, or build knowledge, not simply restate the obvious or provide irrelevant details. If there is a problem, provide a solution. People with a problem rarely need someone to explain their predicament.

40. Be extra careful when writing critical comments – Written works are often distributed to many people and may have a long shelf life. Written criticism can label you as being unhelpful. If you must make a negative or critical comment, try to do so in person or over the phone. Discussion allows the defendant to rebut the statement, and, if necessary, to apologize or make a correction. It also allows you to retract your comments gracefully if your criticism turns out to be undeserved or to have arisen from an error on your part. If you do have to write a complaint, make it constructive by suggesting changes for the better or solutions to the problem that you have encountered.

41. Avoid clichés and overworked words – There are far too many of these phrases and it is easy to avoid them. Many people would probably pay to never hear the word "networking" again. The English language has over one million words; substitute expressions are available for those who look.

42. Use anecdotes and examples sparingly – Anecdotes and examples should be used only to spice up or clarify a written piece. They should not be the main content. Avoid taking the easy way out. Do not tell a brief story in place of making a clear point. Do not use stories, anecdotes, and examples to bulk up your work. The basic message should occupy the majority, not a small fraction, of the total text. Readers will not thank you for wasting their time.

43. **Double-check your math** – Mathematical mistakes are deadly – few things discredit a written piece more quickly. Make sure all of your tables and calculations are perfect. If necessary, have them checked by others. Because math is either right or wrong, and because it can be easily proofed, readers will take errors in math as indications of sloppy work. Math errors torpedo the credibility of your work's conclusions, even when they do not affect your conclusions. Many people can spot errors in complicated math as easily as others spot errors in grammar.

When striving for the highest quality:

44. **Decide who the audience is and then write to them** – We tend to use words in the way we ourselves understand a topic. It is rare, however, for the reader understand the topic the way we do. Compare describing the reliability of a car to an automotive technology class with describing it to your grandmother. Figure out who your readers are and write in their language.

45. **Use multiple editors** – Written works are almost always read by a variety of readers who may come away with different interpretations. The best way to ensure that all of your readers take away the same message is to show your writing first to multiple co-writers or editors. When a number of them agree on the message that you are trying to communicate, a larger number of your readers will receive that message.

46. Practice, practice, practice – Practice makes perfect; the better writers are the ones who write more – those who draft, then rewrite, then rewrite again, and again.

47. Write nice things – Send written thank-you notes, congratulations, and recommendations. These sentiments carry much more weight when written. For extra emphasis, follow up a verbal compliment with a written one.

48. Take the time to be brief – The statement "If I had the time, I would have written you a shorter letter" has been attributed to writers as various as Pascal, Mark Twain, and Ernest Hemingway. This rule of writing clearly shows the direct relationship between effort devoted and succinctness achieved. The easier it is for a reader to understand, the more effective the writing.

49. If you want to write well, read well – The grammar of this old saying may be poor, but the underlying message is true. Those who read a lot, particularly those who read a broad range of literature, including multiple styles and topics, are better positioned to become good writers.

8 insights on wealth management

50. **Save at least 10% of your after-tax income** – Unless you plan to earn an income until the minute you die, you will need to build your savings to carry you (and your dependants) through retirement.

Consider two very different target amounts for these savings.

The easier target is enough wealth so the investment income earned from your savings (post stopping work), plus a gradual depletion of these savings, will support you just up to the point of your passing.

The harder target is enough funds to live off without ever depleting the saved funds. Hit this target and you will never outlive your money and will leave a great inheritance to your successors.

The size of your nest egg depends on three factors: the annual amount you save, the number of years you save that amount, and the income earned on the savings during your working years and before you start depleting them.

Tables A and B below set out the amount of annual savings, as a percentage of your after tax income, that must be set aside and invested over a period of time for you to accumulate the wealth you need to start retirement.

Table A – Investments that will last until your death

Percentage of income that must be invested to achieve a retirement in which continuing investment income plus gradual depletion of the savings will last a limit of 20 years. The boxed square indicates that a person who achieves an 11% investment return and works for 35 years will need to save 8% of their income to be able to continue their standard of living for 20 years after the start of their retirement. After that, they will have no money left.

	Years of Saving / Employment				
	20	25	30	35	40
Investment returns (%)					
7.0	57	42	32	25	20
8.0	47	34	25	19	15
9.0	39	27	20	15	11
10.0	33	22	15	11	8
11.0	27	18	12	8	6
12.0	23	14	9	6	4
13.0	19	12	7	5	3
14.0	16	9	6	4	2
15.0	13	8	4	3	2

Table B – Investments that will last beyond your death

Percentage of income that must be invested to achieve retirement wealth in which ongoing investment income on the saved amount provides for ongoing annual payments and the saved amount is not depleted. The boxed square indicates that a person who can achieve an 11% return and works for 35 years will need to save 11% of their income to be able to continue their standard of living.

ADRIAN PHILLIPS

	Years of Saving / Employment				
	20	25	30	35	40
Investment returns (%)					
7.0	131	97	74	59	47
8.0	89	64	48	36	28
9.0	64	45	32	24	18
10.0	48	33	23	16	12
11.0	37	24	17	11	8
12.0	29	19	12	8	5
13.0	23	14	9	6	4
14.0	19	11	7	4	3
15.0	15	9	5	3	2

These two tables point out one of the most important principles of wealth management: You do not want to outlive your money!

51. **Build your wealth by cashing checks, not writing them** – Building wealth means saving money. Saving money means keeping expenses below your income.

The practice of spending less than you earn is most important in the early days of your wealth accumulation. Consider a person who earns $100,000 per year and has a $90,000-per-year cost of living. This person saves $10,000 annually. Annual investment income on this $10,000 would be in the order of $500 to $1,500. If this person gets a $9,000 raise and uses $4,000 to improve their lifestyle, then the net increase to savings is $5,000. The additional $5,000 saved dwarfs the investment income of $500 to $1,500.

The best way to add to your net worth when your financial assets are small, and you therefore cannot count on earned and retained income on investments, is to increase the amount you save.

Further, it is very instructive to ask yourself, "Should I

spend my energy increasing my income and lowering my cost of living or managing my investment account?" The answer is, "Do whichever generates more cash." (See also #54, below.)

52. Purchase items of high quality, suitability, and durability – Consider the difference between purchasing an auto that costs $20,000 and should last 10 years and one that costs $18,000 and will last six years. The first car has an amortized cost of $2,000 per year and the second car of $3,000 per year. In this case (and there are many like it), the cheaper purchase (the $18,000 car) is actually more expensive. Furniture, appliances, art, and even homes all have this characteristic. The cheaper good that does not last as long costs more per year of usage, not to mention that it almost always costs more to maintain. In addition, better goods are easier to resell should your tastes or requirements change.

53. Understand the three categories of investment – Once you have some savings, the next question is where to invest them. There are essentially three categories:

    (i) Fixed income investments such as bonds, debentures, investment certificates, savings accounts, and preferred shares

    (ii) Commodities such as gold, oil, and orange juice

    (iii) Equity investments such as publicly traded stocks, private businesses, real estate, and similar securities

The *fixed income category* consists of win/lose investments. They take your money and pay you rent (call it "interest"). At some later point, you get your money back. By design, these securities will pay interest that has two components: a portion that will compensate you for the use of your money and a portion intended to offset the expected effects of inflation. When the security reaches its term (matures) and you get your original money back, you either will have won, because inflation was lower than expected and you earned a "free" benefit, or lost, because inflation was higher than expected and you have suffered a penalty for locking up your money.

The organization that sold you this security, however, lives with the opposite consequences. If you win because interest rates fell and you received bonus income, then it lost because it ended up paying a higher financial "rent" than it would have otherwise needed to. If interest rates increase, then you lose and the organization wins by renting your money cheaply.

Thus, every fixed income investment is simply a bet between you and the company on the direction of interest rates. Note here that the organization issuing the security can be a corporation, a municipality, or a state or federal government. What determines whether you win or lose is the economy – something most professionals find difficult to predict.

Yes, these securities are safe, but it is hard to get rich on them. As such, bonds and similar fixed income investments are storage, not wealth-enhancing, devices. They should be used for short-term savings or for low-risk, gradual depletion of your savings in retirement. They are not for long-term building of retirement savings.

Commodities and currency investments offer the same type of bet against the economy as fixed income investments. They can also offer a chance for far greater profits because they have much greater price swings. However, these instruments do not pay any ongoing rent in the form of an interest or dividend payment nor do they add value to themselves. (A company can improve by developing new products and markets or enhancing its operations – gold, orange juice, and oil cannot.) In addition, commodities and currencies with a chance of rising steeply in value also have a chance of dropping steeply in value. Treat them accordingly.

Stocks and equity investments offer a win/win opportunity.

When you buy the stock of a company that goes on to do well, its stock price goes up and you can sell your investment for a profit. You and the company both win. You can even sell your stock to somebody else and they can win when it goes up farther. Yes, stocks do go down and companies do go bankrupt. However, the systemic bias of the corporate structure is to deliver an ever-increasing return to the stockholders. Avoiding stock investment losses, then, is a function of proper selection technique.

54. Choose the person who is best able to manage your savings – An important step on the road to successful investing is to ask yourself, and answer truthfully, two hard questions:

   (i) Do I have the time and skill to effectively manage my own investments?

   (ii) Can I outperform professional money managers?

There is pride and a sense of control in looking after your own investments. But if the answer to either of these questions is no, find someone else to manage your money. Are you able to earn more or save more by pursuing your primary vocation than attempting to beat the market? Many successful lawyers, athletes, entertainers, doctors, and other professionals hand their investment affairs to professional management. They concentrate on what they do best – producing more wealth from their professional efforts – and let other professionals do what they do best – enhancing the value of the investments entrusted to them.

A decision to manage your own money or to let someone else do so does not have to be a permanent one. You can change your mind as your circumstances change, switching from one approach to the other and back. You may also do both – having an expert manage your money in areas where you have little expertise and managing your money yourself in areas where you are sharp.

55. Minimize insurance costs – The average citizen will pay about twice as much in insurance premiums as they collect for any losses suffered. The "missing" half is simply used to pay for the administration of the insurance program. This is not to condemn insurance companies as being wasteful. In fact, most are very efficient. However, they incur substantial costs in running a very complex business and preventing insurance fraud.

Insurance is something that you will need, because there will be times when you simply cannot afford a large loss or are required by law or lenders to have financial protection.

Keep insurance costs low by minimizing the amount of and form of coverage. The most common claims made against insurance companies are smaller claims for less-than-total losses. As such, insurance companies will charge more for the first $1,000 of coverage than the last $1,000 of coverage. For example, you are more likely to dent an automobile than to destroy it. Insuring and administering all of these small mishaps costs insurance companies more. They cover these extra expenses by charging you higher premiums for more comprehensive coverage.

Insure yourself only for the big items and keep your deductibles high.

56. Optimize your borrowings – Few people earn enough annual income to be able to purchase a car or a home by plunking down a wad of cash. They borrow, and borrowing costs can be substantial. Borrowing $200,000 for a 25-year mortgage to buy a home and paying back three $25,000 car loans during the same 25-year period costs about $225,000 in interest payments alone. Simply stated, the added cost of the interest on the loans can effectively double the purchase price of the goods.

Save as much as possible before making the purchase and reduce costs by borrowing the smallest amount necessary. Then, pay back the loan as quickly as possible. Even if you take out a long-term loan, make additional interim payments. Paying down loans early can save years of payments and typically one-quarter to one-half of your total interest expense.

The example below demonstrates the benefit of paying loans down quickly. Assume a loan of $1,000. The interest rate is 6.25% and repayment covers 25 years. Annual loan payments are $80. (Actual loans payments are made monthly but the math holds true in this example.)

The first year looks like this:

Table C

Loan at beginning of year	$1,000
Add: interest costs	62
Less: payments made	80
Loan at end of year	$982

Of the $80 payment made, $62 went to pay the interest but only $18 went to reducing the amount of the loan. The effect becomes more apparent by reviewing additional years, as shown in the next table.

Table D

Year	1	2	3	4	5	Totals
Loan at beginning of year	$1,000	$982	$ 964	$944	$923	
Add: interest costs	62	61	60	59	58	$ 300
Less: payments made	80	80	80	80	80	$ 400
Loan at end of year	$982	$964	$944	$923	$900	

Here, after five years, and $400 in payments, the loan has reduced by only $100, to $900. A full $300 has gone to paying interest. The 25-year picture reveals more:

Table E

Year	1	5	10	15	20	25	Totals
Loan at beginning of year	$1,000	$923	$765	$623	$391	$76	
Add: interest costs	62	58	48	39	24	5	$1,000
Less: payments made	80	80	80	80	80	80	$2,000
Loan at end of year	$982	$900	$733	$582	$335	$0	

This table shows:

(i) It takes 25 years to pay back $1,000 at $80 per year

(ii) It takes $2,000 in total payments to buy a $1,000 item

(iii) The interest costs over the 25-year period amount to $1,000, the same total as the amount borrowed

This purchase will ultimately cost twice what you paid for it.

Table F uses the same math but for one small change – the loan payment has been increased from $80 per year to $105 per year.

Table F

Year	1	5	10	15	20	25	Totals
Loan at beginning of year	$1,000	$815	$510	$99	$0	$0	
Add: interest costs	62	51	32	6	0	0	$569
Less: payments made	105	105	105	105	0	0	$1,569
Loan at end of year	$958	$761	$438	$0	$0	$0	

The difference is material. Total interest costs are now $569 versus $1,000 (before), total payments are now $1,569 versus $2,000 (before), and there are no payments for each of the 10 years past year 15. This gain is simply from increasing the payments.

Even if the payments cannot be increased from $80 to $105 at the start, the same beneficial effect occurs at any time the payments are increased. The magnitude of the benefit is simply changed. Here is the math when the payment is increased from $80 to $102 starting in the 10th year:

Table G

Year	1	5	10	15	20	25	Totals
Loan at beginning of year	$1,000	$923	$796	$498	$96	$0	
Add: interest costs	62	58	50	31	6	0	$843
Less: payments made	80	80	102	102	1	0	$1,843
Loan at end of year	$982	$900	$743	$427	$0	$0	

Now the interest-paid amount is $843 (still less than the original $1,000), the total paid is $1,843 (still less than the original $2,000), and the loan is paid out in 20 years, still avoiding any payments for the last five years. This is a great deal even when you start increased payments later in the plan.

57. Borrow, do not lease – Borrowing requires you to make a higher monthly payment than leasing but decreases the overall amount you spend by decreasing the length of time over which you make your payments. Leasing is simply the reverse of the math provided in the previous item (it extends, rather than shortens, the payment term).

There is also another important difference. When you borrow, you own the car (or item) and the lender is simply renting you money. Thus any car problems are not a major concern to the lender. When you lease, the leasing company owns the vehicle and has a strong interest in how you treat it. If you abuse it, the abuse can become their problem. Leasing companies make up for this risk by charging you more for the lease payments. These lease payments will still be less than the loan payments, but you are paying the lease company for the risk that they are taking. They collect from you by having you pay over a greater number of years. After all, they are in this for a profit.

If you are lucky enough to be able to purchase your first car or home with cash, do not stop there. Continue making savings as if you were making car or home payments. These continued savings will make it less likely that you will have to borrow for any subsequent car or home.

III

Building with People

10 steps to better relationships

58. Strive to be respected by everybody – Develop good and honest relationships not only with your friends and family but also with peers, club members, neighbors, subordinates, co-workers, superiors, suppliers, merchandisers, and customers. Try to ensure that everybody who deals with you would recommend you to others. You cannot make everybody like you, but you can make most people hold you in good regard.

Good people will have healthy differences with you. Ensure that these people are nonetheless comfortable with you. You will seriously limit your own opportunities if you treat others as beneath you or always have an axe to grind with those above you. If you are broadly respected, you will be rewarded with interesting opportunities, free assistance, wise counsel, and good friendship.

59. Treat everybody with respect, courtesy, patience, and interest – This one is really simple and highly effective. The favor will be returned.

60. Do not forget your manners – Say please and thank-you, and do so often. This is one of the simplest and best ways to improve yourself and your situation.

You can demand assistance or you can request it. Requesting (saying "please") is the better approach over the long term. I was once upgraded from a single room to a three-bedroom suite at a ski destination. Why? Because the booking agent left a note in the reservation file that I was a nice person and deserved the best treatment. The hotel desk staff upgraded us on this basis alone and told me so. All I did was treat the booking agent politely.

In a related vein, we often benefit from other people's efforts but are too busy to express appreciation. A simple thank-you, or, as circumstances may suggest, a tangible item such as a note or a small gift, will serve you very well.

61. **When apologizing, repetition is okay** – It is better to use too many apologies than too few. You may think that issuing an apology is an admission of guilt or a display of weakness. But it is better for somebody to say, "You need not have apologized" and think well of you than to mutter, "Why can't this jerk own up to a simple mistake?"

62. **Set modest expectations and over-deliver** – People enjoy pleasant surprises and dislike unpleasant surprises. Have you ever noticed that good restaurants always seat you at a table in less time than they told you the wait would be? Strive to always deliver more than is expected of you.

63. **Place yourself in the other person's shoes** – Much of what you do involves others, so you need to pay attention to how they respond. For example, sometimes people may simply lack your own level of enthusiasm.

The trick is to look at things from the perspective of the person who is looking at you.

Pretend to switch roles. Imagine that the other person is trying to get your support for the idea/concept/request that you are advancing.

For example, if you want to understand how a pregnant

ADRIAN PHILLIPS

woman might respond to your idea, pick up 40 pounds, hold it waist high, and walk around for an hour or so. You will understand her perspective a whole lot better.

Figuring out what pleases, motivates, or annoys others about your project will enable you to describe your ideas and desires in a way that will deliver the best results.

64. Remember that there are two sides to every story/ argument – Every victory, failure, award, divorce, or negotiation has two sides. Try to hear both of them. If you get to hear only one side, do not believe it verbatim.

65. Go for the good people – You will meet thousands of people in your communities and travels, and each and every one of them will possess a mixture of great, good, and bad attributes. Stick with those who have the best attributes. These are the relationships that will reward you the most over time.

66. Always take a positive approach – Every situation has a mixture of good and bad. Find the good in the situation and make use of it or build on it. To the extent that the negatives can be ignored, do so.

67. Build long-term relationships – We often build a relationship around a short-term event, perhaps a project, visit, or shared experience. In cases like this, strive to keep the relationship on good terms even if it may be somewhat dormant because the reason for the relationship has disappeared. Avoid being a relationship hunter, trading one relationship for a better one as opportunities may arise. Be selective when building relationships and then hold them for the long term.

10 hints on dealing with others

68. **Encourage people to talk about themselves** – Most people want to talk more about themselves and listen less to you. You will succeed greatly in your endeavors by letting others talk more about their business, their detailed requirements for your services, and even how they would do things if they were in your shoes. The same goes for social gatherings. Make people feel at ease by discussing things that are familiar and pleasurable to them instead of trying to impress them with your favorite opinions and topics.

69. **Avoid situations that create embarrassment** – Most of us will do almost anything to avoid even the slightest embarrassment. When you are with one or more people, or in a public situation, be sure not to embarrass anyone or put them in a situation where they may be forced to embarrass themselves. Negotiations, promotions, and social or business exchanges can be wrecked when one person feels in danger of being embarrassed. Try not to corner people.

Stated more positively, help someone avoid embarrassment and you may make a friend for life.

70. **Understand the individual's underlying motivation** – It has been said that if you do not understand a situation, then look for any financial interests that may be involved. This expression can be expanded to a broad variety of situations. Look hard for people's "personal interests." Close observation of their individual motivations will explain their reactions to many situations and will help you predict outcomes.

71. **Ask for forgiveness instead of permission** – Often people with control like to exercise it just because they have it. When you suspect that something you wish to do may be quashed as a result of this kind of territorialism, forego asking permission and forge ahead on your own. In most cases, since there really was little reason for them to say no anyway, permission will be proven to have been unnecessary. If you *were* wrong, ask for forgiveness. Either way, you have clarified your position.

72. **Pick the best spot to mount a challenge** – Do not try work on too many fronts at one time. Many people consciously or unconsciously resist allowing another person to take most or all of the cookies from the jar. Furthermore, your ability to wage several campaigns at one time or a very complex campaign will tax your abilities. It is easier and often more effective to navigate a sequential campaign instead of several campaigns at once.

73. **Win people to your cause by helping them measure their risks** – Many situations in life involve some degree of risk. Most people will proceed and cheerfully accept the consequences (whether good or bad), but only if they can estimate the risks before they start. Everyday examples include pushing a stroller across an intersection, investing money, driving a car on a snowy highway, or launching off a diving board.

However, people usually avoid risks that they cannot measure – they assume that non-measurable risks are large risks. This is often why you cannot persuade your spouse, co-workers, or friends to join in with your plans. Remember, it is not your assessment of the odds and consequences but *theirs* that matters. They will not join you unless you give them access to all of the key facts in your possession.

74. Build support, *early*, through shared experiences – You will be faced with situations in which you are the primary or sole person responsible for a task or for seizing an opportunity. Often you will require the support or approval of a colleague or superior or perhaps a group of colleagues. It can be very difficult to get them to break away from their own priorities and prejudices.

The trick is for you to get one or two people involved with the key details of your project. Get them involved early. This can be as simple as asking them to participate in an office or factory tour, inviting them to a meeting with a few key counterparties, or seeking their assistance with a section of the analysis.

By having a colleague work alongside you on part of your efforts, you may gain good independent guidance. More importantly, the colleague may be just the informed and vocal supporter you need when you must ask for approval from your organization.

A different, but clear, example of this phenomenon is starting a family. Many people's best and longest friendships are with those in their circles who started having children at the same time they did. Meeting the challenges of those high-demand early years together creates very strong bonds.

75. Sell on the positive, not the negative – You will encounter situations where you want somebody to select your charity, method, or product over somebody else's.

Take the approach of speaking mostly to the *merits* of
what you are offering. Show them the benefits that your
proposal will deliver to them. (Avoid negative comments
about competing proposals – even if your comments are,
in fact, true.)

For example, seek donations by emphasizing that an
individual's contribution will help cure heart disease, not
by stating that heart disease is more important to cure than
kidney disease. Negative comments turn people away.
Positive comments attract support.

76. Never underestimate the need for personal trust

– People prefer to deal with people they have had the
opportunity to meet and assess first-hand. Much of what you
do in your daily life can be done efficiently and effectively
among strangers and even without personal contact. More
important matters require the support of people you have met
and deem worthy, knowledgeable, and helpful.

Example? Selecting a dentist. Selection criteria
typically include location, friendliness of staff, educational
achievement, professional accreditation, chair-side manner,
expected fees, and a suitably equipped office. However, a
good dentist provides a very pleasing result, and a poor dentist
provides a very painful result. You would travel out of your
way, deal with a crabby receptionist, ignore the certificates
on the wall, endure a boring personality, accept the use of
older equipment, and pay more money for a dentist you can
trust completely to deliver a bright smile, healthy gums, and
protection from pain.

That said, service providers seeking to build trusting
relationships must make sincere efforts on the basic items.
The best technical dentist in the world has to master some
amount of chair-side manner and keep some semblance of
an appointment calendar or risk losing patients.

77. **Know where to place your trust** – Judging where to place personal trust is another matter. We can be deceived by a service provider who returns phone calls quickly, promises free delivery, makes emergency appointment time available, and remembers small details … but fails to deliver on our true needs. Be careful not to be schmoozed on peripherals and shortchanged on key deliverables.

IV

Interacting with Others

15 basics for advancing in groups

Self-improvement also includes improving how you get along with others. No matter how excellent you are, you still need a team or the cooperation of others to achieve anything of any merit. Maximize the way you relate to others within your organization and elsewhere.

78. Do your own job best – You will be graded almost solely on your ability to carry out your own set of responsibilities. Resist the temptation of telling colleagues how you could do their jobs better, or worse of trying to do their jobs for them. You will most likely fail and be labeled a meddler for your troubles. If you do succeed, you will be seen as lucky. Either way, you will detract from your own responsibilities and expose yourself to errors and weak performance in the areas where you are being more closely observed.

79. Stay highly organized – An organized person is a more effective person. While it can be thrilling to fly fast and loose, all too often oversights occur, things get done poorly, and quality suffers. Take it as fact that you will not be rewarded for sloppy or partial delivery of your own responsibilities. However, you will be promoted for effective and proper performance of your duties. Organized people also have the time to see opportunities and possibly create new and better things.

80. **Treat those below you as you treat those above you** – Treat your subordinate the same as your boss, your supplier the same as the customer, and the volunteer the same as the benefactor. You will get better performance in return. Who knows, one day the subordinate might be your boss, the supplier your customer, or the volunteer your benefactor.

81. **Make the pie larger, not the slice** – Think of rewards in your organization as the pie and your share as a slice of the pie. If you want a bigger slice, do not go after someone else's slice but work to make the pie larger. Better to have good-sized piece of a larger pie than a larger piece of a smaller pie.

82. **Do the small things** – While you will not want to make a career out of assisting people in small ways, you should be humble from time to time. This includes getting a coffee for your assistant, helping the maintenance man move that heavy item, or doing some small but helpful chore for your boss. If you can eliminate an embarrassing or awkward situation for someone by doing a simple job outside your job description or position, do it. People prefer associating with real human beings, not status-oriented fusspots.

83. **Help the weak** – Do not think it goes unnoticed when people teach weaker or newer colleagues or otherwise help them to better perform their duties.

84. **Show, do not tell** – On a scale of one to ten, boasting about a specific capability is worth two and demonstrating your capability is worth nine. This is why the quiet, competent person is more successful over the long haul than the horn-blower.

85. Make decisions – Professional money managers are highly successful if they pick outperforming investments 70% of the time and underperforming investments 30% of the time. You can learn from this. You are not expected to make a perfect decision every time. You simply have to make well-reasoned decisions. A well-reasoned decision that does not pan out is not a mistake – it is simply an event that has unfolded in a manner that you did not desire.

86. Be quick to correct your mistakes – You should recognize a bad outcome when it occurs and not be shy about making a change. Your first loss is often your smallest loss. Make a correcting decision. Do not waffle or procrastinate.

87. Lead by example – Do the things that you want your employees/colleagues/fellow volunteers to do. If you want them to work long hours, you must work long hours. If you want them to penny pinch, you must penny pinch. If you want them to give to charity, you must be charitable. If you are lazy, flamboyant, or extravagant, your employees will follow your lead, to the detriment of your organization.

88. Build experience as your most valuable asset – Companies or customers pay people for getting the job done. While you may enjoy being on a steep learning curve in a job, know that this constitutes a downward profit curve for your employer because it is getting less value for the paycheck it gives you. Developing the experience that you have gained elsewhere in your company or career will enable you to quickly and efficiently fulfill your responsibilities with little supervision and at the lowest cost to your employer.

Get as much experience in your area of focus as you can. This, along with your thinking skills, is what you were hired for.

89. Take risks but do not be reckless – Higher levels of responsibility will be granted to you if you can demonstrate an ability to:

(i) Carry out your responsibilities and/or capture an opportunity

(ii) Avoid anything that could retard the opportunity

A few mistakes are acceptable; recklessness is not. Too many mistakes cannot be offset by even a very high number of good deeds. If you cannot be entrusted to carry out a function with care, you will be held back from more challenging and rewarding roles.

90. Mimic the dog that trots about and finds a bone – Luck most often finds the person who is there to receive it. The real estate agent who sells the most homes is highly likely to be the person who knocked on the most doors, made the most presentations, distributed the most listing flyers to mailboxes, made the most phone calls, made the most follow-up calls, and got to know the most buyers and sellers.

91. Work harder and smarter – Our ultimate success is a product of our contribution. You can make your contribution more valuable by working harder or working smarter or both – which is a lot easier than trying to increase your intelligence.

92. Always contribute – One way or another, occasions in which you deliver 110% performance, help a colleague, volunteer for a dirty job, or simply avoid being critical of a bad situation will be factored into assessments of your success in an organization.

6 ways to better climb the ladder

93. Be clear about your aspirations – Make sure
your superiors know where you would like to go in the
organization. Much management time is wasted trying to
figure out ways to motivate and challenge employees or
volunteers. Being open on this subject will make your boss's
job a lot easier. This does not mean being openly ambitious
– that can often lead to overly competitive staff situations or
the development of unrealistic expectations. Your superiors
benefit from this information, but your colleagues will not.

Choosing how to tell your superiors about your desires is
fairly simple. Pick a time for sowing the seeds when there is
no need for action of any kind. Find a time and location where
the discussion comes up naturally and is private – for example
sharing a car or airplane ride or going out for a quiet lunch.

94. Compete with competitors, not teammates – Many
people play the game of internal politics, wasting energy to
prove that they are better than their colleagues rather than
spending it on achieving a win for the organization. On a
10-point scale, outdoing a colleague advances you by one
point, outdoing a competitor by seven.

95. Beware of hidden factors that will influence your path – The decision to promote an individual, grant a pay raise, award a contract, or add to job responsibilities is rarely made by one person. Typically the person who tells you the good news has consulted several others and checked your history.

It is those "others" who can propel, or limit, your opportunities. For example, that "moron" you embarrassed may have just been asked if they would be willing to work for you in a new capacity. You will not be asked to attend these types of discussions and will not have the opportunity to defend yourself.

Do not underestimate the impact of these discussions; a "no" vote from somebody you have offended will limit your chances. Similarly, enemies within your organization often become your clients or superiors. Be good to everyone and have no enemies. If you find an enemy, try to negotiate a peace – or at least to achieve a ceasefire by achieving mutual respect.

96. Match authority to responsibility – Many seek higher levels of responsibility as a way to advance their career. Be certain that your authority is increased when your responsibility is increased. If the level of authority is too low, you will not be able to do what you need to do to meet your increased responsibilities. This sets you up to fail. Mismatches in which too little authority is given for the amount of responsibility expected are very common. In fact, many organizations seem almost biased toward setting things up this way. This mismatch is a leading cause of career failure. Watch for it and avoid it. When offered an opportunity that has more responsibility than authority, you do not have to decline it. Simply insist on more authority.

97. Identify your replacement – Your ability to move on to new and better roles will depend on your abilities, the availability of opportunities, and, additionally, someone to replace you. You should identify and nurture one or more replacement candidates to insure that you are not held back when an opportunity to move forward presents itself to you.

98. Move ahead by waiting – One path to a promotion is to simply wait. At one point or another, the seniors in your organization will themselves be promoted, quit, be fired, or retire. These events create an opening for you. If you are doing well, you will be considered favorably for the opportunity. Many an impatient employee left just a little too early, throwing away the promotion they were about to receive.

7 measurements to determine if an organization fits you

99. **Assess the culture of the organization** – Collectives of people develop their own mannerisms and culture. These can range from welcoming and supportive seniors homes or hospitals to the feeding frenzy shark tanks of some large corporations. Even entities in the same business can have differing cultures. Find a culture that meets your desires and makes you feel comfortable. It is almost impossible to change an organization's culture once it has been established. It is easier to change organizations.

100. **Determine where you stand among those around you** – Often within a group of people who share a common mission, some will try to advance themselves to the detriment of others. Watch for those who wish to run over you. You are there to pursue the primary mission of the organization but may have to defend yourself against some colleagues. Minimize distractions arising from wasteful internal competition.

101. **Seek exposure that will broaden your perspective** – Many potential superstars are unaware of the vast array of lifestyle and career choices available to them. Many people who have not yet begun their work life or who live in a sheltered or quiet environment are limited in their life choices by the breadth of their parents' and friends' vision. To the extent that you can broaden your exposure to a wide variety of careers, do so with vigor. This requires legwork and hustle. You will find that many people are only too happy to spend a bit of their precious time explaining their particular line of work. Just ask them. You will learn about a wealth of opportunities.

102. **Play on a team that is aligned with your skill as a player** – Always strive to be an "A" player on an "A" team. Assess yourself honestly to see if you are an "A" player on a "B" team or a "B" player on an "A" team. Both are acceptable and can position you well for the future. However, if you feel like a "C" player on a "C" team, you are in a rut and need to make a change.

103. **Benchmark yourself against what you could do on your own** – Many people choose to avoid an organization or a particular culture either by working on their own or creating a new organization. This can be a highly rewarding and very effective. It is always worth benchmarking yourself against this alternative.

104. **Look at the entire package** – People seek a career primarily because the role matches what they are trained to do or like to do – for example, "I trained to be nurse so I will take a job in nursing." This is a good start but is far from the only criterion involved in the decision. Stability, potential for advancement, location, benefits, and many other factors should also have an influence. Decide how important these factors are to you before signing on.

105. **Adhere to the FIFO principle** – FIFO simply means "fit in or fly off." You should plan to support the organization's game plan or leave. Resisting that plan will sap your energy, generate ill will, and mark you for ejection from the team. Do not try to fight your organization unless you are absolutely certain you can make it change – which, by the way, typically has a one-in-a-hundred chance of happening.

1 time-tested rule

106. **Be prepared for a change of organizations** – No matter what your occupation – whether you are an insurance agent, manufacturing manager, charity booster, athlete, business person, entrepreneur, administrator, or teacher – you should expect a change of organization sometime in your future. You may make the change in search of better rewards or perhaps your organization will part company with you. Prepare for such eventualities by:

(i) Keeping yourself marketable so you are desirable to others inside and outside your organization

(ii) Being aware of other opportunities

(iii) Continuously upgrading your skills and education

(iv) Being honest about your skills so you can properly (and happily) fit into a new position

(v) Keeping a strong communication network with others outside your organization

17 ways to win with colleagues

The most important asset for any charity, any educational institute, any government department, any service organization, any business, at any time, is its people. At some point, you will likely be asked to lead a team, or be part of a process that selects a team. When this occurs, your main concern will be attracting and retaining the best people.

The benefits of having strong people are legion. Good colleagues take less supervisory time. They innovate. They sell better, gather support better, and build better. They create fewer problems and deliver more to the organization. They attract other highly capable colleagues. The list goes on and on.

107. **Learn how to spot the winners** – Your organization's success will be clearly related to the ability of the people its people attract. Spotting winners is easy. When conducting an interview or reading a résumé, look for people who:

   (i) Have a propensity for action. Choose people who initiate things themselves

   (ii) Pursue leisure activities that advance them. Look for people who, for example, pursue arts or sports opportunities in their spare time as opposed to those

who devote their time to watching superficial
TV programs

(iii) Have achieved academic excellence. You do not have
to find people with 4.0 GPAs or who scored 1450 on
their SATs, but do try to source those with "A" marks,
particularly across a variety of studies

(iv) Follow a solid reading program. Look for people with
a record of meaningful reading, because this kind of
reading indicates a desire for self-improvement

(v) Have competitive or leadership instincts. Look for
people who took a lead role in the local fundraiser,
have played on winning teams, have captained the
debate club, or have served as student council president

(vi) Have diverse interests. Find people who pursue a
passion, contribute generously to a charity, or study
topics beyond their everyday experiences

You can count on it: The way a person contributes to your
organization will flow from their general approach to life.

108. Know the five reasons that people pursue a regular activity:

(i) For income and to build their net worth

(ii) For a feeling of partnership or teamwork

(iii) For intellectual challenge

(iv) To compete and win

(v) To build a better world or for charitable purposes

Nurses and other health-care professionals are primarily
motivated to make a better world. Astrophysicists are in it
for the intellectual challenge. Commissioned salespeople
want to compete and build income. Police and firemen are
team players.

Ask new applicants for their own personally desired balance among these five items and compare what you hear with what you think can be achieved in your organization. Hire people who want to do the role you wish to fill. Matching them to what the organization can offer makes for the best staff additions. Mismatches create high turnover.

109. **Be big by talking about big topics** – You can judge people's character by observing what they talk about the most. Small people talk about people. They tend to be shallow, gossipy, less committed, intense. Big people discuss events, accomplishments, philosophies, strategies, and the like, and they tend to make better employees, friends, and colleagues.

110. **Pay for the best** – Hire the most capable people even if they cost more. The very strong employee who costs 20% more will provide more than 20% increased value to the organization. They do this through better performance and by requiring less management. If cost is a limiting factor, hire a less experienced "up and comer." Hiring such people will provide much more to your organization than hiring a slow-growth journeyman will. If you are a volunteer organization, strive to attract and retain the best by providing them with the best roles.

111. **Source new employees based on the attributes they already have** – When hiring, you can often extrapolate from the candidate's prior role(s). People who have been in the work and volunteer world for many years are unlikely to change when they join your organization. Stars will continue to be stars and journeymen will continue to be journeymen. It is uncommon for a "B" grade contributor to convert into an "A" contributor upon joining your group.

All you have to do is consider professional sports. The list of mediocre running backs in football who have been converted into all-stars is a fraction of the list of mediocre

running backs who remained mediocre after being traded
to a new team.

112. **Transcend the 2-6-2 effect** – The 2-6-2 effect can apply
to any group of people (employees, teammates, volunteers,
etc.). In essence, 20% of them will perform their function with
great success and require little supervision; 60% will achieve
good success and respond to the organization's improvement
efforts; and 20% will likely do a poor job – they will draw a
disproportionate amount of coaching energy and not improve
from it.

Your role as a leader of a group is to provide sufficient
resources to the top 20%, guide and support the next 60%, and
trade, upgrade, or remove the last 20%. Strive to build a 2-8-0
or 3-7-0 environment.

113. **Do not hire a good geologist; hire a lucky one** – This
old adage points to the fact that some people have a natural
gift for what they do. Their résumé may not be filled with lists
of academic achievements, industry citations, or progressive
increases in responsibilities. However, look closely for a
record of overachievement in their particular field. Some of
the most boring or difficult people you meet may also become
your most competent colleagues. Sometimes it is difficult to
explain why an individual is so good but their results easily
justify keeping them on the team.

114. **Employ people to do what they want to do** – You can
lead a person to water but you cannot make him drink. It is
hard to motivate people – whether by compensation, favorable
recognition, or reward – to do what they fundamentally do
not want to do. Recognize these behavioral limitations early
and you will save yourself tons of effort. Employ people who
personally want to do what you want them to do. Reassign
those who are not in the right spots.

115. Remember that motivation may work more narrowly than you expect it to – People like to think of themselves as being sophisticated, broad-based, long-term performers but often spend most of their time chasing short-term goals. Employees will be highly motivated to achieve simple, singular goals that benefit them, even if achieving them is to the detriment of the organization.

Take the example of commissioned sales. An organization that tells employees that their paycheck is going to be a fixed percentage of their sales had better establish an effective set of cost controls. In the absence of controls, no expense will be considered too great by an employee intent on securing that all-important sale and therefore a fatter commission check. You can be sure that the employee will spend plenty of the company's money to wine and dine the prospective customer. Guard against this.

116. Remember that a penny to the company is a dollar to the employee – Things that are small or trivial to the organization can be very important to the individual. Consider pay cuts. Taking $100 off an employee's pay may not represent a large saving to the company but will have a negative effect on the employee – possibly causing them to quit. Organizations waste vast amounts of wealth when they get these things wrong. As a rule, expect people to give up very little, even if they are being asked to give up the tiniest of things; anything they consider "earned" may as well be considered sacred. For proof, look at this phenomenon as seen in the public marketplace. Have you ever known a tired and ineffective government social program to be eliminated or downsized without a public outcry?

117. Do not expect leopards to change their spots – You will come across people who lack in moral fabric or are dishonest when under pressure, especially when their income or image is at risk. Do not believe that such people will change or will desist from such behavior in the future. You know from experience that people who deceive will do so again. Avoid these people in your day-to-day life and part company with them at first offense. In these situations, your first loss will be your smallest loss.

118. **Realize that a pause means no** – Offer a person an opportunity they like and you will get quick acceptance. Offer them one they do not like and they will often start to analyze and stall in giving you a response. A pause generally means no. If you get a yes after a period of time, be careful that it was not given because the person does not want to disappoint you. Hand-wringing and deliberation can be a waste of time and energy.

119. **Over-challenge your subordinates** – Good colleagues revel in greater challenges. They see them as an opportunity for growth. In addition, giving them extra responsibility is a good way for you to discern high-caliber colleagues from good-caliber colleagues.

120. **Hire top performers when their employer stumbles** – It is difficult to persuade high-performance employees/ volunteers in other organizations to leave their current roles and work for you. Their organization will do anything to keep them satisfied. It is a different matter, however, when their organization makes a mistake. Note, though, that you are more likely to persuade them to join you in these situations if you have built a relationship with them over time so they are comfortable with you and your organization and have been presold on the opportunities that you can provide.

121. **Use the best, not the mediocre, as points of comparison** – We tend to rate and rank our own staff relative to one another. This is dangerous. If our organization has a weak staff, we end up merely making distinctions between levels of mediocrity. It is better to compare staff with a competitor's staff. However, do not feel comforted that your organization is on par with others. Rather, source people who are the best in their fields and make them your point of measurement. This is what the professional sports teams do.

122. **Import fresh perspectives** – Imported talent is a benefit. While companies typically strive to build better colleagues from the rank and file, a few select imports can bring a fresh perspective, as well as information on how other organizations or competitors function. Importing people also demonstrates to existing staff that individual capability is as important as loyalty for career advancement.

123. **Choose people who walk on escalators** – There are two kinds of people – those who stand on escalators and those who walk on escalators. Ask yourself which category each of your prospective or current team members fits into. You will immediately identify those you should keep, because they seek to over-contribute, and those you should part company with, because they are just along for the ride.

25 tips on speaking and listening

Effective verbal skills will help you get things done your way and make a great impression on the people who can help propel you forward. Whether you are at work, in the community, or at home, effective communication is one of the more important skills for you to master. The fact that you know the solution, have a powerful insight, or are able to improve a particular situation is of little use if you cannot communicate what you are thinking. Being able to listen is as important as being able to speak.

Some things to emphasize:

124. Keep it simple – When you speak, select words that convey a clear message. Cover just a few key points. Most listeners can absorb only one concept at a time and only two or three concepts during a lengthy conversation. Any more than a few crisp messages will confuse them. If you must convey a complex topic, use visual aids.

125. Ask open questions – Avoid questions that have yes or no answers. Do not ask, "Were you born in Philadelphia?" Do ask, "Where were you born?" You will get a richer answer.

126. Know what you do not know – It is easy to get caught up in the excitement of a conversation and be drawn into areas where you have little knowledge of the topic but feel you have to say something. Avoid this mistake. Say something only when you can have an impact. Otherwise, simply sit back, especially when the discussion turns to areas where you are not so smart. There is a lot that is good and little that is bad in saying "I don't know" or "Can I get back to you on that topic?" Sometimes it is better to remain silent and appear to be a fool than to open your mouth and remove all doubt.

127. Communicate often – Keep people up to date with your activities and the status of what you are doing for them, and ask them how they are doing. Regular communication builds good relations; sporadic or no communication creates distance.

128. Say it once – A properly emphasized statement needs to be stated only once. Repeating yourself only diminishes your point and may cause you to be seen as argumentative. If what you are saying adds to the conversation, then people will remember it. If others in the conversation ignore what you are saying, let them. They may be disagreeing with you silently or may believe that the comment is out of context or naïve. Repetition can be annoying. Do not try to re-plow tilled soil. (Notice how the message in this paragraph came simply from the first line?)

129. Be sure to listen more than you talk – People are often set at ease by talking about themselves, their families, their desires, and their accomplishments. Encourage this type of conversation. You learn very little when you do the talking. Let others do most of the talking. This is the best way to get value from the conversation. Also, you will put the other person at ease and give them a memorable, enjoyable experience.

130. **Always be confident, even when you are not perfectly correct** – Strive to project confidence in everything you say. It is okay to be confident when you are mostly correct; however, be careful not to cross the line, exuding confidence when you are not really qualified in a matter. You do not want to bruise your credibility.

131. **Do not be afraid to say no** – If the situation is clear and simple and warrants a no, then just say so. On many occasions, the fear of hurting somebody's feelings by saying no results in a misleading response, and this can lead to wasted effort and time. Being forthright is a virtue. If you mistakenly give a no answer, you can turn the no into a yes. It is more difficult to turn a yes into a no.

132. **Learn how to say no without saying no** – Sometimes an outright no can cause damage. People dislike hearing no and may react badly. The trick is to learn ways to say no without making things personal. The most famous of these is the "I have to wash my hair on Saturday night" line used to refuse an offer for a date. When asked to propose on a business opportunity that you do not want to pursue, you can simply quote a price for your services that you know will be rejected.

Other methods include stating that you lack the time or resources to fulfill the request, or that you have a conflict because of other dealings. You may be faced with a situation in which the request is highly personal, such as, "Can I borrow your fancy antique sports car?"

Often the reason for saying no is personal; in the last case it may be a concern about the person's history of reckless driving. You may be better served to express your inability to deliver on the request than to explain why you are saying no.

133. **Convert presentations into two-way conversations** – Presentations are typically made to gather support or to sell someone on an idea or to sell goods or services. Get your audience to tell you what they want. Discussions are often better than lectures. People want to talk about themselves, their business, and their needs. Listening, knowing, and understanding build trust in your audience. Some of the most successfully delivered presentations are ones in which the recipients did more than half of the talking.

134. **Tell all, tell it early, and tell it yourself** – When there is a problem at hand, take leadership in communicating it. Do not try to hide or slip away from bad news. Be tactful, but let people know the whole story.

135. **Voice your support early** – If you wish to support a person who is trying to win a point, then join in quickly. This builds momentum. It helps forestall others from banding together to contradict.

136. **Conduct listening checks** – Sometimes it is very helpful to say back to the person what you believe they have said to you. This technique will help you sort out complicated or unfamiliar topics.

137. **Match your greeting to the type of meeting** – Determine the nature of a particular gathering and act accordingly. Trying to be funny during serious or grave occasions can make you appear insincere. Overuse of charm in an organizational or business setting can make you look slick. Intense shoptalk at a social gathering can make you appear shallow or narrow. Show some charm when hosting, be gracious to newcomers, show sympathy in times of sadness, and talk about business in business settings.

138. **Match the venue to the conversation** – Need a place for a private, uninterrupted conversation on a touchy subject? Go for a car ride together. Want to bestow some form of flattery or recognition with a little more impact? Do it in front of a small group. Want to yell at someone? Do it where no one will notice that you are mad or that the other is being scolded. Need to negotiate something tough? A phone call is better than a series of emails. Do you have bad news? Try to deliver it in person and in private. You will get much more out of communications when you match the venue to the type of message.

Some things to minimize:

139. Do not speak when listening – You may be tempted to make your views known by being first, using the most words, or trying to be the center of attention. In most circumstances, do not rush in. Let others speak; watch where the conversation is leading and see how others are reacting. You can reform your thoughts or choose more powerful words after digesting other speakers' messages. When you turn comes, speak in a crisp, competent manner. In conversations you are judged by the quality, not the quantity, of what you say and not in the order in which you speak.

140. Be aware of body and facial gestures – People speaking to you deserve your full attention and your sincere desire to understand what they are saying. Give them anything less and they will likely treat you poorly when it is your turn to speak. Make sure that you do not listen with a grimace or in a laidback posture with your feet resting on the table and your hands behind your head. Similarly, pay particular attention to the expressions of those you are speaking to. Facial and body language give clear signals of receptivity and may indicate the need for a mid-conversation alteration.

141. Avoid using profanity – The use of profanity in general conversation, and especially in workplace conversations, is a waste of words and reduces the listener's respect for the speaker. Yes, there are times when a well-placed swear word or emotional outburst will enhance your message. However, conversation littered with profanity diminishes the speaker. Think of the expression "the difference between poor and successful people is that successful people do not swear."

142. Do not answer questions for others – Some people feel compelled to answer a question that is not directed to them; they may feel they have a better answer, or worse, they may want attention. When people ask someone a question, they are seeking that person's opinion, interpretation, or knowledge of the facts and not yours, even though you may have a better response. Additionally, respondents find it presumptuous of you to answer questions for them; they feel they are quite able to answer for themselves. You can offend both sides with this behavior.

143. Do not translate other people's communications – Unless asked, never try to simplify and restate what another person is trying to tell an audience. It makes both the person and the audience feel they are being treated like idiots and makes you look as if you consider yourself to possess a higher level of intellect.

144. Do not ask an important question unless you already half know the answer – When you are counting on a specific answer to persuade a group, make sure you have a sense of what the answer will be.

145. Never disrespect someone's spouse, religion, employment, or politics – It is all too easy to spot somebody else's shortcomings or decide that your whatever is better than theirs. It probably is not, and even if it is, you are still going to get an argument.

146. **When you find yourself in a hole, stop digging** – If you have made a mistake or insulted someone, or are simply on the wrong side of a conversation, then stop. Apologize, correct yourself, or back out. Do it quickly, cleanly, and sincerely.

147. **Be very selective with the media** – The press, radio and TV, and the Internet are all places where you can easily lose your focus and ultimately your prosperity. People are drawn to the media like moths to a flame and the result is often the same. While it is fun and personally rewarding to see yourself or your organization in the public eye, consider that the media:

(i) Rarely compensate you for the information you provide

(ii) Control the message or content of what you are stating

Also, members of the media are experts at what they do and you are a novice, or at best a part-timer. Why would anybody subject themselves to this set of circumstances? For some exposure? This is a bad tradeoff.

The media are masters of extracting information. The lengthy comments that you provide in fine detail will be distilled into one or a few phrases with much of the meaning distorted or lost. You may find that some catchy but uncomplimentary or inaccurate phrase may be attached to you that you have little ability to shake off. Always remember that not answering gives the media nothing to report. Often those who cannot avoid the media have media handlers.

Unless you can control, or are compensated by, the media, ignore the media. If you feel compelled to repair poor reporting or wish to set the facts straight, speak to the media on the basis of full anonymity.

148. **Make the extra effort to leave a good impression**
– It takes only two intelligent comments to leave a good impression and only one dumb comment to leave a bad one.

V

Optimizing Yourself

10 ways to be more efficient

149. **Devote your energies on the basis of impact** –
Everything you do has benefits and costs (time, effort,
money, etc.). Choose activities on the basis of the best
personal benefit for the least personal cost. Asking somebody
who is more capable to do a chore for you may be smarter
than undertaking it yourself. Think of homeowners who
attempt their own complex repairs instead of calling in
better-equipped and more capable professionals.

On the other side, doing some things yourself is often
easier and more efficient than asking someone who is poorly
positioned to do so. Example? Never ask somebody to write
a condolence letter for you.

150. **Treat time as your scarcest resource** – On a typical
day you will sleep for seven to eight hours, perform bodily
functions (eating, personal hygiene, etc.) for a couple of
hours, travel for an hour, devote three hours to family and
friends, and spend eight hours in core activities such as raising
your children, school, employment, contributing to a charity
or community, or helping friends and relatives. This leaves
two hours per day for personal development and all of those
other miscellaneous things. No one has found a way to expand
time, so it is very important for you to make the most of these

few precious hours. Plan your use of time carefully – wasted hours can never be recovered.

151. **Touch things only once** – Strive to complete tasks without interruption. Both time and effort increase when you start and stop a job repeatedly before completing it, particularly if the task requires you to re-familiarize or re-equip yourself every time you start again. Consider painting a room. Time is wasted if you repeatedly set up and take down ladders and clean and reuse paintbrushes. Saving time and energy by doing tasks in a smooth, continuous motion will give you more time for the important things in life.

152. **If you cannot find one, make one** – Necessity is the mother of invention. You should not let the lack of something get in your way. Improvise, substitute, create, and jury-rig to get things done.

153. **Get to it and knock it off** – For all regularly recurring events, deal with them crisply and well before the next occurrence. Read today's newspaper today (or no later than tomorrow). Pay this month's bills soon after they arrive. The principle is simple. There is less value in reading last week's newspaper than in reading today's. Unpaid bills do not go away. They simply clutter your life until you take care of them. Worse, if you pay them late, they accrue late charges and cost you more.

154. **Watch for collateral outcomes** – Much of what you do is directed at achieving a single desired objective, whether buying a car, winning a game, or finishing a project. However, life is not simple. The achievement of an isolated objective may have unintended consequences.

For example, that extremely hard negotiating tactic that got you the lowest price on a refrigerator may come back to haunt you in the form of a grumpy delivery person or terrible warranty-related service.

Similarly, switching to a new but higher-paying job in a particular field may drop you into a cutthroat corporate atmosphere or prove to have been a "desperation hire" before a looming, but hidden, bankruptcy. When you set out to achieve something, consider what the softer and often hidden effects may be. They may arise from the process that gets you there or may have been hiding in wait for you all along. Be careful; these can be very material.

155. Be calm when others are stressed – You can accelerate your effectiveness when the effectiveness of others is deteriorating. When circumstances create pressures or limit time and resources, many will falter. This is when you should avoid the distractive nature of the situation and focus on the facts, opportunity, or problem. A calm, focused approach will propel you forward when others are lost or frozen. Many intense situations seem to beg for a jolt of emotional energy (which can be exciting for you and the participants), but calm, clear thinking and smooth, deliberate actions will win the day.

156. Think of tasks in units of happiness – The objective of most of what we do is to improve something. An improvement ultimately means people are happier. When approaching a task, think of the goal as a prize measured in units of happiness. This will help you tailor your approach and determine which resources to use.

157. Figure out how to give when taking – All of us are happy to take something if it is free. However, the situation is quite different if somebody wants to take something from us – for example, reducing one of our benefits or no longer providing us with something that we have grown accustomed to. If you have to take something from somebody, try to find something that you can give in return that will at least partly

offset the loss. Otherwise, too much of your energy may
be spent dealing with a highly disappointed person or group.

158. **Remember that girlfriends/boyfriends are like
subway cars** – The expression "If you miss one, then simply
get the next one" has often been used to guide a younger
individual to move on (and quickly) when recovering from
one of those early, painful romantic failures. It is an odd
expression but can teach you that putting the past behind you
and pursuing future opportunities (yes, many will come your
way) is the more efficient way to advance. Moving on will
keep you from getting stuck in a situation for which there is
no repair.

3 thoughts on passion, hustle, and energy

159. **Identify the factors that influence outcomes** – Any situation, problem, competition, or project includes a number of factors that will influence the outcome. It's important for you to assess these.

In a situation with 10 factors, the person with a mastery of nine of them is much more likely to beat the person with a mastery of eight. Examples abound:

(i) The local restaurateur who has cleaner premises, better food ingredients, and friendlier and faster service will do better than the haphazard operation next door

(ii) The high school teacher who dedicates additional energy to lead the school play will advance better than the equally capable teacher who does not

(iii) The well-rehearsed, well-equipped, and talented musician will outperform the well-equipped, equally talented, but less-rehearsed musician

This point is simple but many ignore it. Many people stop when they have learned six of the ten factors. The more committed go on to eight. The successful do not stop at that level but go on to nine. If you want to be successful, keep going until you have mastered the fine points or delivered that little bit of extra effort.

160. Be aware that others are judging or measuring you – You are being judged all the time. Judgments range from your mother-in-law's assessment of your cooking skills to your boss's take on your work ethic to a golf club's assessment of your social skills. In these judgments, you are compared with others.

Life is full of comparisons (and in many situations, competitions); maximizing your success means moving ahead of others when measurements are being taken.

161. Competition can be invisible and much different from what you think it is – Competition (and comparison) in day-to-day life differs from what we typically expect or have been trained to look for. Why? Because the competitors and their actions are not fully visible.

Competition as generally recognized involves a one-on-one or team-versus-team situation with a preset playing arena and a fixed set of rules. Each competitor can see the other's movements and can measure performance with statistics or on the scoreboard.

You will not see much of this open, level-playing-field type of competition in your day-to-day world.

For an example of hidden competition, consider what really goes on when you collect money for a charity. The people you approach likely are known to give to charities. They will have their own views on the worthiness of your charity relative to many other needy organizations. When you ask for a donation, say, to a cancer research organization, you will be competing for dollars against other disease charities. You will also be competing for dollars with other organ-related charities.

And competition will also come from a multitude of social causes, such as deprived children, the destitute, the elderly, and the addicted, not to mention Third World charities.

Be aware that competition likely exists in all of your endeavors.

27 plays for your negotiating playbook

The world runs on exchange and trade. Be thankful that most trade is simple and requires little or no thought or action. However, you will come across many situations, including car or house purchases, antique or charity auctions, purchases of goods or services, or even community efforts, in which what is paid and what is received are not preset. When the amounts become large or the stakes are high, you can count on a negotiation.

Do you need to negotiate?

162. **Determine first of all if a negotiation is required** – Many of life's exchanges can be completed more easily and more quickly by avoiding a negotiation. Negotiations often take on a competitive spirit that has more to do with who wins than with achieving goals. This chews up energy. Sometimes making a generous first proposal or accepting someone else's first proposal will allow you and the other party to get on with other higher-value activities or avoid wasted effort. Negotiations begin when a counterproposal is made, not when the first proposal is made. Be certain that a counter-response really is better than a yes in getting you to your ultimate goal.

163. **Sometimes you should be pre-emptive** – Sometimes it is best to start off with a take-it-or-leave-it offer, for example if the other side is motivated to transact but is unaware of, or worried about, the number of parties that may be competing for the opportunity. In these situations, strike with a clean and fair offer and drive to close as soon as possible. Try to cut off any attempt by the other side to get an auction going and enhance what they receive in the exchange. The prospect of a quick, clean, and fair deal may compel the other side to transact. They may do this out of fear of losing your proposal or to avoid a time- and energy-consuming auction process.

Before you start to negotiate:

164. **Plan on negotiations ending somewhere in the middle** – Successful negotiations end with two results:

(i) The exchange of something with a value for something different but with similar value

(ii) The retention of pride

Negotiations can be lively (on the part of both parties) over the measurement of the relative contributions. However, a breaking point is often reached when one side feels that they are losing face because they feel there is no win in it for them.

165. **Remember that negotiation is not solely about winning** – Negotiation is about achieving an arrangement that meets with both parties' objectives. You should always try to let the other side feel that they are taking away a win, so long as you have met your minimum objectives. This should lead to a speedy and simple conclusion that minimizes competitiveness and hostility – the two things that waste the most time and energy.

166. **Figure out what the other side wants** – What they want may differ a lot from what you think they need.

If you know what they want, you may be able to pay less (or provide less) than what you would otherwise pay by altering the components of what you are giving.

For example, an individual selling a business that they built may want an ongoing role in the business, in addition to a cash payment for the sale, out of pride in building the business or a difficulty in parting from it emotionally. You may be able to offer less cash by offering the owner a seat on the board of directors, an ongoing consulting role, or passive involvement in management.

167. **Know which of the three main negotiation players you are bartering with** – In any negotiation, you can be dealing with one or more of three counterparties:

(i) The messenger

(ii) The decision maker

(iii) The executor (the one who delivers the goods)

The messenger conveys the information back and forth between you and the decision maker. They have no authority in the process.

The decision maker determines the outcome of the negotiation.

The executor upholds their party's side of the completed barter.

Observe whether the roles are split among several individuals. People sometimes fail in a negotiation by trying to get the wrong things from the wrong people.

The decision maker is the person you want to deal with. You can spot a decision maker by determining who has the power to commit their side to the bargain. Confirm that this is the case and then find out what they want, make them feel that there is a win in it for their side, avoid embarrassing them, and conclude the deal.

Never, ever, negotiate with the messenger. You can spot a messenger when you see that they have no authority to commit to a deal. They may pretend to have authority, but they do not. They will often try to get you to improve their position by making statements such as, "The manager will not accept that; we need more." The most common example of a messenger is the car salesperson who always has to check with the boss.

Messengers are a ploy to wear you down. You can be tricked into letting them have too much of a role by feeling that as human beings they are (or should be) a meaningful part of the process. Do not let sympathy get in the way. There are two ways to deal with a messenger:

(i) Install your own messenger to offset their advantage

(ii) Limit the messenger to delivering your words in the negotiation to the decision maker and informing you of the decision maker's responses

Make sure you know who will execute the work or delivery that you have negotiated for. Obtain comfort or assurances that good delivery can be made. For example, you may win a negotiation in setting up a contract for a renovation but receive substandard work or materials because the folks performing the job are unhappy with the terms their team leader got for them.

168. **Get your facts straight** – Negotiations are basically an exchange of facts that result in the exchange of goods or services for money. Knowing exactly what you want to accomplish, the value of your proposal, and all of the selling features for your side of the exchange are the keys to a successful negotiation. Even better is knowing the value of the other side's proposal and the selling features of its goods/ services.

Negotiating from a position of strength does not mean

yelling louder or arguing longer (although these tactics do have a role from time to time); it means convincing the other side, based on a better knowledge of the facts, that you hold the stronger position.

169. Do not fight precedents – There will be occasions when you will be seeking what appears an easy "give" for the other side but find them highly resistant to conceding the point. What you are asking may seem small to you but large to them because giving it to you may require them to give it to many others in their future negotiations.

A great example is commissions on real estate sales. Asking a realtor to reduce their commission by, say, $300 may seem reasonable to you given a home sale of several hundreds of thousand of dollars and therefore a commission to the realtor of several thousand dollars. However, what appears to be $300 to you, appears to be thousands of dollars to them – $300 times each and every future sale.

170. Limit the time allowed – People with lots of free time may treat a negotiation as a game, arguing over microscopic details and/or trying to renegotiate previously agreed-to terms. Before initiating a negotiation, decide how much time should be required. If there is a deadline, and the items to negotiate are few and simple, start the negotiation shortly before the deadline. If you start weeks earlier, you may find yourself devoting weeks of time and resources with little, if any, incremental benefits.

Tactics, process, and setting terms:

171. Set a reasonable first offer – One key to a successful negotiation is to set out a reasonable first position that will encourage the other side to proceed with you. If you are selling, your price must be low enough to get their attention but high enough to reflect reasonable value to you. If you are buying, your bid must be high enough to get the vendor's attention but low enough to reflect good value to you. Stray too far from these parameters and you can expect one of three results:

(i) The other side will ignore you and you will have wasted your efforts

(ii) You will enter into an overly lengthy negotiation that will waste time, money, and energy, or

(iii) The other side will drive a much harder negotiation in order to "get even" for your initial lack of commitment to a fair and balanced process

Being spotted trying to pull a fast one is costly. You may receive a proper pummeling or be forced to discontinue the process until the circumstances change and the parties are prepared to try a fresh start.

172. **Know who is getting skinned** – If you do not know who is getting skinned, then you are the one getting skinned. Offers that are too good to be true, negotiations that seem too easy, or products and services that demonstrate some form of magic usually mean that you are not grasping the entire picture. Be sure to understand what all parties are giving and receiving in the exchange. Follow the old adage for poker games – if you cannot spot the sucker after five minutes of play, you are the sucker.

173. **Strip out the emotional content** – Negotiations should be all about exchange, not about excessive ego, winning versus losing, or flamboyance. It is all too easy for these matters to become a large factor in a negotiation. Try your best to stick to the facts. Other than being sensitive to any need to minimize embarrassment (discussed earlier), keep things clinical.

174. **Strive to be condition free** – Some people dislike negotiations and essentially want to make the transaction and get on with other business. You can get more out of such a negotiation by attaching few or no conditions to your position. In other words, make it easy for the other side to agree to your terms.

The most common example is to offer cash with no contingencies based on financing. It may be simple for you to arrange financing, but the other side does not know this because they lack a detailed knowledge of your finances. When selling, be capable of providing delivery immediately so the purchaser can receive instant gratification.

175. **Never negotiate against yourself** – Negotiations are exchanges of information and should be back-and-forth exchanges. If you provide some information, expect and receive something in return. If you make an offer, do nothing until you have received a counteroffer in return. The party that can make the other side improve its offer without providing a counteroffer in return is the party that controls the negotiation and will ultimately come out ahead.

176. **Let the other side talk first** – You are better off if the other side states its views first. Although *you* should never negotiate against yourself, do not stop the other side from doing this. Let them do most of the talking. People often want to be the first to express their views and may not realize that doing so is commonly a disadvantage in a negotiation. If the other side wants to go first, let them. If they are too eager, they may offer too much right off the bat. You may just find that their initial proposal exceeds your ultimate expectations. You may be able to negotiate an even better deal.

177. **Know that you cannot dictate, you can only educate** – You should be well prepared and well equipped to convince the other side of the merits of your proposal. Sometimes, however, this preparation leads to an overly high level of conviction. The result is an effort to dictate to the counterparty that they should do what you want. This is a really good way to wreck a negotiation. The result is typically lost value for your account. The other side will have its own views and will have to make up its own mind. Pushing too hard can damage your position.

178. **Avoid having to retract** – Once you have offered something in a negotiation, you can retract it only if you offer more of something else. Lowering your bid in a negotiated process is an act of bad faith and will frustrate the negotiation.

If the other side lowers its bid, discontinue the negotiation. Accepting their tactic will categorize you as weak and you will suffer for it.

179. **Distinguish between tangibles and deliverables** – The purchase of a tangible good is a simple exchange of your money for an item of defined specifications. If the specifications of the item are well known to you, and fixed, you can drive hard on price and achieve good value.

This is not the case with deliverables. With deliverables you pay money for some future delivery of a service or a package of tangible goods. In this form of purchase, you must be certain that the other side walks away from the bargaining table satisfied (or better yet, happy). If they are not satisfied, you will not be satisfied with the deliverables. The vendor will attempt to rebalance the exchange after the deal has been agreed by reducing their contribution.

For example, squeeze a building contractor too hard on price and the work quality will suffer – and probably in a way that you will not notice until long after you have parted company.

***180*. Ignore the bluster when it comes to fair market value**
– I sold my dog for $50,000; I took two $25,000 cats for a
trade. Negotiations frequently involve participants sprinkling
the discussion with indicators of value such as "I have already
been offered $ [an amount larger than the amount under
discussion]" or "A friend of mine sold a very similar (but
different) item last month for $ [a large amount]."

Ignore this bluster. The definition of fair market value
is "the price at which two arm's-length parties will conduct
an exchange as expressed in money or money's worth."
Any vague or imperfect comparisons add little value to
a negotiation and thus should carry little weight in the
discussion.

If you are taking a non-cash item as part, or all, of the
payment, then the true value of your sale is the value that you
would have to pay to separately buy the non-cash item, what
you would receive if you were to sell the non-cash item, or
the item's personal utility value to you.

***181*. Listen to the silence** – A skilled negotiator will remain
silent on topics that are secondary to the transaction at hand
if they have the strength to take advantage of these items at
a later time. You should not assume that certain items will
follow or are assured because "they normally go that way."
If there is silence on a particular topic, plan on receiving
nothing with regard to it.

***182*. Set down all of the terms before accepting** – Always
know, and if necessary put on paper, the terms of the
negotiation. All of the terms. In addition to price, the terms
should include timing and method of payment, specifications,
and the exact nature of the good or services and their
availability. Open items (after the negotiation is finished)
rarely work out in your favor. The other side is unlikely to
do anything or agree to anything that has not been written
down or clearly specified.

Look at how the experts do things. Have you ever wondered why banks are so particular about the paperwork and fine points before they lend money? It is because borrowers rarely think about anything beyond paying the loan back once they get the money and buy the item. They are not inclined to deliver copies of insurance papers, sign promissory notes, and deliver similar important documents once they begin enjoying their new goods. Experience has taught banks that leaving things open-ended leaves them open to losses.

And most importantly ...

183. Complete negotiations as friends – Strive to complete any negotiation in a friendly and win/win manner. Whether you feel that there is a win for you, you should negotiate the deal so the other side feels they are carrying home a win. People are much easier to negotiate with when they think that they are winning as the process evolves. Importantly, you may have to negotiate with the person again or they may be in a position to deliver a future benefit to you.

184. Stay friends after a failed negotiation – If you cannot agree to terms, having tried to do so with care and patience, then break off negotiations graciously. You never know when a party may come back to the table or you may wish to revisit your offer. As is commonly said in business, "Things changed." This may include new factors in either party's situation, abilities, or desires.

Other types of negotiations and how to deal with them:

So far this section has dealt with the most common type of negotiations: those between you or your team and another person or team. From time to time, you will be confronted with different types of negotiation frameworks. Most of the suggestions above will apply, but the "fit" will seem different.

Following are descriptions of and strategies for four other types of negotiations.

185. **Distinguish between the interests of the individual and the organization** – The resistance of the other side increases when they are bartering for their own wallet rather than for their organization's wallet. Many corporate purchases are completed when the buyer agrees to provide a few extra million dollars. That same buyer may be the type who refuses to spend an extra thousand dollars to purchase their own new house even when the price is below local market prices.

The most difficult situation arises when the interests of the larger organization are being negotiated against the interests of the individual. Take the seemingly small interests of the individual seriously. Not doing so typically results in a highly emotional and unproductive session.

186. **Make good on difficult three-party negotiations** – Situations will arise when there are three parties to a particular negotiation. While three parties can often find common ground for a transaction, there are two types of situations that can be very good or very bad for you.

One type is when two of the parties get together to create a stronger deal for themselves. Obviously being part of a double-team effort is far superior to being the victim of one.

The other type is when one party plays another party against the third party. This is the old divide-and-conquer strategy. In this case being that first party is more effective than being either of the other two parties.

When entering into multiple-party negotiations, analyze each of the players and assess your ability to take a position of strength. Also assess the possibility of being forced into a position of weakness. Be aware that positions can change during a negotiation. For example, if you are the recipient of a double-team attack, you should seek to divide the attackers.

If you are forcing two other parties to bid against each other, be aware that one may form an alliance with the other as a defense mechanism. Always keep these options in mind and do not hesitate to adopt them yourself during the course of a negotiation as circumstances may require.

187. Determine who you are really negotiating with – Before you start, find out whether you are negotiating on a one-to-one or one-to-many basis. One-to-one situations in everyday life include car purchases, home sales, and the like. One-to-many situations come up when someone is trying to sell an item or many of the same items to a large group of possible buyers.

In a one-to-many situation, you are denied the ability to negotiate with each individual and thus are basically forced to commit to a price that meets the criteria of the lowest-paying member of the group. Selling a weekend getaway vacation package to a group of five couples who will divide the expense is a good example. The important price is not the highest one that any single couple will pay but the price that the "cheapest" couple will pay.

Your objective in a selling-to-many effort is therefore not to seek out the highest single bid but to remove any negatives that the lowest bidder may have. Alternatively, you may succeed by attracting such a large population of buyers that you can ignore the low end of the group. The remaining group is still large enough to meet your selling amount and price targets.

188. In bidding competitions, stick with the maximum you are willing to pay – You may be faced with a situation in which you are forced to bid against several others for an item you desire. Examples include furniture or art auctions or home purchases. In some cases, such as in live auctions, you will be able to see and challenge the other bidders. In other cases, such as in closed auctions, you will get only one or two chances to submit a bid and will not see what other bidders are bidding. The key to winning is to know the maximum amount that you are prepared to pay.

For most people, this maximum amount is based not on mathematical calculations but on emotions or gut feel. Instead, think of your maximum price in terms of "if a competitor paid $xx and won the bidding contest, would I be mad for not matching or exceeding their bid?" Your answer tells you the maximum you are willing to pay. You likely should move quickly toward bidding this amount.

Many opportunities are lost because people try to get something too cheaply instead of thinking more about what they really want.

11 TAKEAWAYS

189. **Design your own personal goals for success** – Know where you are starting from, figure out the resources you are going to need, pick a speed, and go. Be adaptable along the way. Make adjustments as necessary. Reach your targets. As you proceed, your targets will change and evolve. This is good; it means you are meeting your early targets and moving on to higher ones.

190. **Assess yourself candidly** – Adopt some new and better personal habits. Improve on the ways that you currently handle yourself. Strive to do fewer things but do them to a higher standard. Pursue the five elements of excellent health: a high-protein, high-fiber, high-vitamin, and raw-foods type of diet; lots of fresh air; healthy doses of sunshine; lots of exercise; and meaningful rest.

191. **Polish up your communication skills** – Add to what you learned in school. Your communication skills should all be top-notch.

192. **Understand and manage your finances to live within your means** – Design and build a wealth-accumulation program. Be prepared to take advantage of wealth-building opportunities when they arise. Save at least 10% of your after-tax income.

193. Conduct your affairs on the basis of their impact – Make more time available by being highly organized. Work smarter, try a little harder, and put in more energy than others into each and every situation.

194. Understand how and why organizations are the way they are – Figure out how to navigate through organizational mazes and the people you encounter there.

195. Be aware that comparison and competition surround you – This is true even if you do not like it. Keeping alert to how others might measure you will enable you to advance toward your goals with greater ease.

196. Build stronger and more permanent relationships with others – Always be a positive contributor. Do your best to be respected, and liked, by everybody.

197. Develop insights into how and why people behave the way they do – Learn to spot people's behaviors and react well to them. Put people at ease so they can enjoy the experience; avoid embarrassing them; and leave them feeling that they have achieved something by being with you.

198. Seek ways to make exchanges good for both sides – Do your homework and be well prepared for major purchases and negotiations. Strive for win/win situations and to complete all encounters as friends.

The one most important thing:

199. Be content – You can influence your destiny and happiness and the happiness of those around you. Figure out what you want. Attaining success means determining what you want from life and then organizing your life to achieve and enjoy these things. Some people want many things from life and some want little. Many contented people are not wealthy, wise, or at the top of some pyramid. They know what they want from life and have arranged their affairs accordingly. You can do the same.

CPSIA information can be obtained at www.ICGtesting.com
Printed in the USA
LVOW132315200612

286980LV00019B/43/P

9 780988 035201